BYRON

BROADWAY

CHARLIE

CLAUDE

CALIFORNIA

COLIN

CRICKET

DIGBY

ELPHABA & JOSEPHINE

WOOF

**To Koko
and Cricket**

Hoop n Loop

CAROL TAI

Hardie Grant

BOOKS

The Projects

Small Breeds

Large Breeds

Medium Breeds

Introduction

As a child, I was obsessed with animals. I grew up in the dense city of Hong Kong, where my family lived in a small apartment with no outdoor space, so it wasn't practical to have any pets. However, when I turned nine, everything changed.

I went to boarding school in the English countryside, far away from friends and family. The school had a labrador called Buddy, and we soon became good friends. Buddy and I would go for walks, and I'd spend hours sketching horses in nearby fields. Eventually, my family moved to Scotland and after much persuasion, I finally got a dog of my own, a Border collie called Koko.

Fast forward into adult life. Having graduated from Manchester Metropolitan University in Fashion Design, I became a pattern cutter working in London. Pattern cutters translate the sketches made by designers into patterns, which are used to make samples. Working in the fast-fashion industry is pretty intense, so I took up embroidery as a hobby to de-stress.

At first, I struggled with the embroidery world as it seemed quite old-fashioned, and hand embroidery required more patience than I possessed. I started lots of projects, but hardly had time to finish any of them. But then I discovered freehand machine embroidery and

quickly fell in love with it. This doesn't require much skill and it is so much quicker than stitching by hand. There's a whole community of creative people pushing this craft forward today, which I think is fantastic.

After a while I was looking for new embroidery templates to try out, and decided to test making some of my own. But what to create? And then my worlds collided – I started making patterns featuring Koko.

That Christmas I made everyone in my family a Koko embroidered cushion and they loved them. Word soon spread, and other family and friends were asking if I could make something for them. Eventually I started receiving requests from around the country, from people I didn't even know. In 2017 I established my business, Hoop n Loop. Since then I've created hundreds of unique embroideries of people's pets. While it has been hard work, I feel very lucky to have combined my passions.

I'm very excited to be able to share more of this incredible craft, and my love of dogs with you, in this book. I hope these projects bring you as much joy as they did me.

Carol Tai

How to Use This Book

This book is pawfect for any dog lover who would like to have a go at creating some exciting embroidery, whether you are an experienced freehand embroiderer or this is your first attempt. This book is intended to guide you through the projects step by step, so get ready to have some fun. Remember, these projects are meant to be enjoyable. If you get overwhelmed or frustrated at any point, just take a deep breath and go back to it when you are ready.

Freehand/free-motion machine embroidery is like drawing with your needle, so with some practice and a little patience, anyone will be able to make any of the projects in this book.

Before you start any stitching, it is important to make sure your sewing machine is set up correctly, so please read the information on pages 28–31. You may also find the tips and tricks on page 34 useful, especially if you are a beginner.

When you are ready to start, find your favourite dog breed in the project section. Each project will give you a list of colour embroidery threads needed and roughly the amount of time it should take you. Feel free to change any thread colours to customise the look of the embroidery. This is your embroidery, so let your imagination run free.

Select your garment and you will find all the templates at the back of the book or online at www.hoopnloop. co.uk/templates. Follow the step-by-step instructions to create your embroidery. There are no hard-and-fast rules, so you can swap garments/fabrics for each project if you wish to do so. This book is only intended to be a guide and a starting point for you.

Basic Techniques

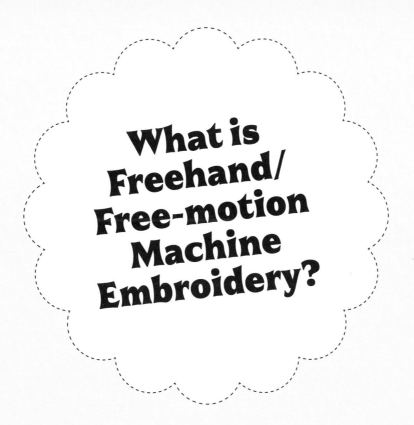

What is Freehand/ Free-motion Machine Embroidery?

Freehand/free-motion machine embroidery is a fast, accessible and fun way to create exciting embroideries at home without having to invest in expensive embroidery equipment. All you need is a normal domestic sewing machine, as well as a few tools, and you are ready to start creating some fun embroideries.

Freehand machine embroidery gives you the total freedom and control over the stitch direction and you can even stitch curves, flowing lines and wiggles, which in this case is ideal for stitching different fur types. It is like doodling with your sewing machine, using needle and fabric instead of pen and paper.

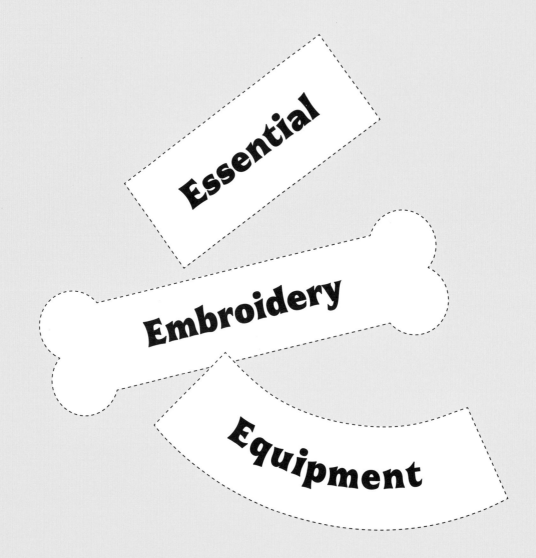

Essential Embroidery Equipment

One	**Sewing machine**

A sewing machine designed for craft and dressmaking at home is ideal for creating projects in this book. There are many domestic models available, and at many price points, so be sure to do some research before buying. You want a good, heavy-duty machine, and I like those manufactured by Singer and Janome. Some are more advanced than others and include features for many different stitching styles and techniques. These can be helpful if you are an advanced sewer, but straight stitch and zigzag stitch are all you will need for the projects in this book. See page 28 for advice on how to set up your machine.

Two	**Free-motion embroidery/darning foot**

A foot is the metal plate which sits around the needle. The purpose of the foot on a sewing machine is to hold the fabric flat while sewing.

A free-motion embroidery or darning foot is a spring-loaded metal foot which allows it to bounce slightly when sewing. It can be easily changed and fitted to most sewing machines. The free-motion embroidery/darning foot can vary slightly in appearance depending on the model of your sewing machine, but all of them have the same function, which is to allow you to stitch freely in many different directions. This foot is often not included when purchasing a basic sewing machine, but it is widely available and very affordable. See page 30 for instructions on how to change the foot on your sewing machine.

Three	**Machine embroidery needles**

The size of the needle varies between 70 and 110 mm. The lower the number, the finer the needle. The size of the needle required depends on the type of fabric, stabiliser and thread use. A suitable needle size is recommended at the beginning of every project. However, for most fabrics, size 70/80 embroidery needles will be just fine.

For stretchy fabrics, I recommend using a ballpoint needle, also size 70/80. Ballpoint needle tips are rounded to allow the needle to pass between the threads of the fabric without ripping or damaging it.

| Four | **Wooden hand embroidery hoop** |

This is optional, but strongly recommended for beginners to help with stability and for work that is going to be heavily stitched.

Embroidery hoops come in all sizes ranging from 7.5–35.5 cm (3–14 in) and can be found in most craft stores or online. Ideally, use a hoop which is 2.5–5 cm (1–2 in) bigger on all sides of the design you are embroidering.

For most of the projects in this book, I recommend a 30.5-cm (12-in) embroidery hoop so the entire design can fit within the hoop and there will be no need to reposition during stitching.

| Five | **Stabiliser** |

A good stabiliser, sometimes called backing, is used to support the fabric during the stitching process. It prevents the fabric from puckering or stretching and can also help to keep stitches intact, thus prolonging the life of the embroidery.

Stabilisers come in many different weights and forms, and there are so many to choose from. In my experience, tear-away or water-soluble stabilisers are the most effective for the projects in this book, but it is always best to test a few different stabilisers with the fabric you choose to use and find the most suitable.

Tear-away stabilisers are temporary and generally easy to remove or 'tear away' once the embroidery is finished. I recommend using tear-away stabiliser with all embroidery projects, no matter the fabric.

Water-soluble stabiliser is a clear plastic-like film, designed to dissolve when wet. This is great for free-motion embroidery as you can draw or trace your design straight onto the stabiliser to create a stitching guide. Some fabrics might be difficult to mark or trace on to, even through a light box – in this instance I use Sticky Fabri-Solvy by Sulky. This water-soluble stabiliser allows you to stick your transfer directly onto the material, preventing it from moving around.

For thicker or non-stretch fabrics, using the tear-away backing is sufficient. However, if you are stitching onto a thin fabric or stretchy fabric, I would recommend using both tear-away *and* water-soluble stabilisers. Sandwiching the fabric inbetween stabilisers makes it less likely to move while stitching (the tear-away is placed at the back, and the water-soluble at the front or on top).

| Six | **Heat and bond ultra iron-on adhesive** |

Some items are tricky to embroider onto, so it might be a good idea to stitch the embroidery onto a separate flat piece of fabric, similar to a badge. This paper backed sheet iron-on adhesive is an easy way to attach the embroidery badge.

<table>
<tr><td>Seven</td><td>

Fabric marker pen

A fabric marker pen is used for drawing on to all fabrics, from cotton and polyester to leather. The ink can be permanent or non-permanent (which can be removed after stitching) and comes in many different colours. Alternatively, a simple pencil will do the job.
</td></tr>
</table>

Eight

Embroidery scissors

There are many visually appealing and beautiful embroidery scissors available, depending on your budget, but the most important consideration is to find a pair you are comfortable with. Make sure the pair of snips you choose have small, thin, pointy tips. The blades must also be sharp enough to allow accurate cuts to tightly stitched areas without damaging the fabric underneath.

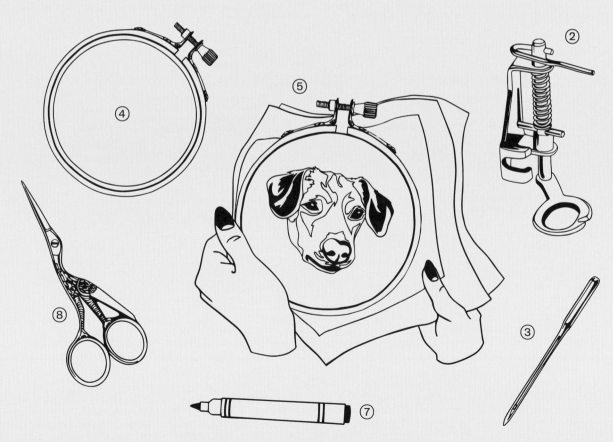

Fabrics and Threads

One	## Fabrics

Embroidery can be machine-stitched on to almost any prewashed (to avoid shrinkage) fabric. However, until you are more confident, try to avoid very thin or stretchy fabrics. Light, flimsy fabrics are rarely suitable as they cannot take the weight of heavily stitched filled areas. Very stretchy fabrics are difficult to work with – not only will they move around while stitching, but they also have a tendency to pucker with dense embroidery stitching.

Non-stretch cotton, canvas and linen are considered some of the safer fabric choices.

Two	## Clothing

Most, if not all, of the embroidery projects in this book are stitched on to ready-made garments. Instead of buying new items of clothing, try upcycling. This is a great way to transform second-hand garments into something wonderful and unique, while avoiding waste as much as possible. Fast fashion is a growing concern for the environment, so being aware and making little changes can help drastically. Furthermore, embroidering onto old garments is a creative way to spruce up your wardrobe.

Three	## Embroidery thread

For both free-motion and computerized embroidery, it is essential to use a good-quality machine embroidery thread which will ensure great results every time.

Rayon or polyester thread has a beautiful high sheen and a natural glossy finish. These threads are super durable and will withstand washing at 95°C (203°F), making them perfect for using on clothing.

I am a huge fan of Madeira embroidery threads. They have an enormous choice of threads, ranging from classic colours to neon, frosted matt and metallic threads. Madeira embroidery threads are great quality and can be purchased worldwide. If you really want to go crazy, Madeira has a range of twisted threads, containing different shades of browns or greys. These shades are twisted into a single strand of thread, creating interesting textures – perfect for making your dog embroidery come alive.

Standard cotton thread does snap easily when used for freehand or free-motion embroidery. It is not strong enough to withstand the jerking motion when stitching, making it less suitable to use for our pet-portrait projects. Some cotton threads can shrink and some of the colours might even bleed when washed, eventually ruining the embroidery design. For these reasons,

I don't recommend using it for the projects in this book.

In terms of thread quantities, a 2.5-cm (1-in) square of embroidery uses roughly 160 cm (63 in) of thread. However, more precise quantities are given within each project.

When embroidering large areas in one colour, it's easiest to start with a fairly full spool of thread (save emptier spools for embroidering small details, such as eyes, noses, etc.).

Four

Embroidery bobbin thread

This is a lightweight, almost clear thread specially designed for any machine embroidery use. The bobbin thread is strong enough to withstand the stress of any high-speed stitching, yet fine enough to prevent a densely embroidered design from being too stiff, dense and rigid, while allowing layers of threads to be laid over each other.

You could use bobbin thread in a colour to match the embroidery thread. However, if there are eight different thread colours in a single design, this would mean changing the bobbin eight times. In addition, the end result might be denser and bulkier.

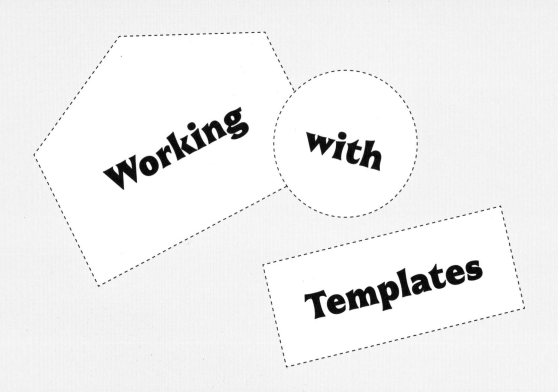

Working with Templates

For beginners, it is always best to sketch your design on the fabric first before doing any stitching, to avoid mistakes. You can use a pencil or a fabric marker to draw straight onto the fabric if you are sufficiently confident, or you can trace the design using the template provided for each project.

I recommend using a light box to trace the template, but if you do not own one, simply place the template and fabric against a window (tape them to the glass to hold them in place) – the daylight shining through works in the same way as a light box.

All the project templates are approximately the same size. However, they can easily be resized by using a photocopier. Alternatively, the templates can be downloaded from the website www.hoopnloop.co.uk/templates.

Tracing

Tracing is the most common way to transfer a template on to clothing. Simply trace straight on to your clothing by placing the template underneath one layer of fabric, and use a pencil or fabric marker to trace the design. If the fabric is thick, use a light box or a window.

Water-soluble stabiliser

Drawing on to water-soluble fabric stabiliser (see page 20) is an easier option when using thicker fabrics, like denim. Transfer your template onto the stabiliser by tracing with a pen. When this is done, peel off the backing and stick directly onto the clothing where you would like to have the embroidery. When the embroidery is completed, simply dissolve the stabiliser in lukewarm water.

Template resizing

To resize the templates in the back of the book, you can calculate the percentage it will need to be scaled up or down by depending on the embroidery size given in the particular project and the size of the template. Alternatively, you can scale it up or down according to the specific garment you want to work with. This can be done by photocopying the template at your chosen size, or by downloading the template (see opposite) and printing at your desired size.

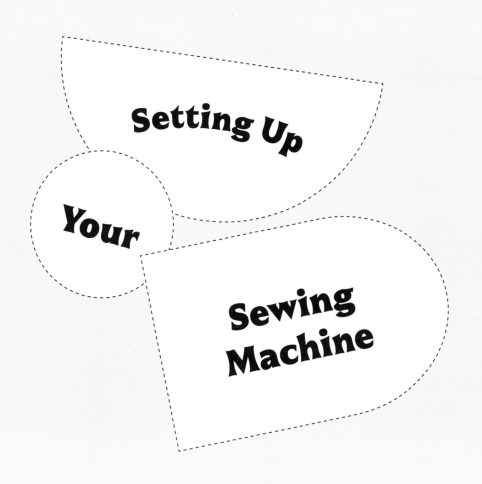

Setting Up Your Sewing Machine

Before doing any freehand/free-motion embroidery, you must make sure your sewing machine is set up properly.

One	**Lower the feed-dogs**

The feed-dogs are thin metal crosscut teeth that sit under the sewing machine's needle plate. Lowering the feed-dogs is very important as it will allow the fabric to move in any direction, rather than restricting the movement to only forwards and backwards. To disengage the feed-dogs, there is normally a switch at the back of the sewing machine, but each sewing machine model is slightly different, so check your manual if necessary.

If your machine does not have the option to lower the feed-dogs, you can buy a special plate to cover them. This will work well, but the cover will not sit flush on the bed of the sewing machine, so pay attention to this when stitching to ensure your work does not get caught or snag.

Two	**Attach the free-motion embroidery/darning foot**

Once the feed-dogs are lowered, change the foot on the machine. The pressure foot is a metal attachment which sits around the needle. The foot acts like a guide, holding fabrics flat while stitching. A lever (usually found behind the foot) controls the foot's position, it must be down while stitching and lifted up while removing any fabrics.

First remove the original foot by unscrewing it – you will need a screwdriver to do this on most machines.

Once removed, replace with a free-motion embroidery/darning foot. Remember to tighten the screw after changing foot, making sure the claw-like part is secured around the metal bar. This now allows you to move the fabric freely while stitching. To test the free-motion embroidery/darning foot is secured correctly, lift the lever up and down a few times to make sure it does not fall off.

Three	**Change needle, if necessary**

There is no right or wrong time to change a needle. Usually a needle is only replaced when it breaks. However, every time your needle goes through the fabric, it causes micro-wear on the point, making the needle less sharp so it is harder to go through the fabric. A blunt needle not only skips stitches while sewing, it can sometimes rip the fabric, creating big, visible holes with each stitch. For these reasons I recommend using a new needle for each project as this is a very simple step to ensure your project runs smoothly.

To change needles, make sure the foot lever is up. Then simply turn the knob on the right-hand side above the needle with your fingers or screwdriver. The old needle should fall out. Then replace with the new needle and tighten the knob.

Four	**Thread your machine with embroidery thread**

All sewing machines should have diagrammatical instructions on how to thread them. These are often shown on your machine and in the manual. It is just a matter of running the thread on the spool pin through to the needle by following the thread guides on the machine. Use embroidery threads for the projects in this book to achieve best results (see page 23).

Five	**Change to embroidery bobbin thread**

Place a spool of embroidery bobbin thread on the spool pin and place the empty/new bobbin on the bobbin winder shaft. The winder shaft is usually placed on top or at the right-hand side of the machine. Follow the instructions in your manual and fill the bobbin with embroidery bobbin thread. Then place the bobbin back into the compartment below the needle. Remember to replace the bobbin case cover if the machine has one.

Six	**Set the stitch length**

Set your straight stitch length to zero as your own stitching action will determine the length of your stitch.

Seven	**Test the tension**

It is always a good idea to make a few lines of stitch on a spare piece of fabric (similar to the fabric being used in your project) to test the tension. The correct tension stitching is flat and smooth on both sides and the interlocking of the threads sits midway through the fabric.

Tighten the tension knob if the stitching loops show on the underside of the fabric. If the stitch loops are showing on the topside, loosen the tension knob. Be gentle when turning the tension knob. Usually, a tiny twist is all you need to fix the problem.

Eight	**Get creative**

Now your machine is ready for freehand/free-motion embroidery. Get creative and, most importantly, have lots of fun.

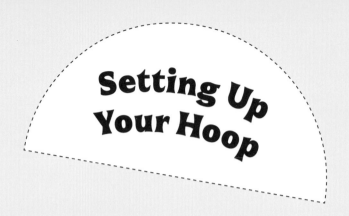

Setting Up Your Hoop

It is vital your fabric is safely secured in the hoop and does not fall out during stitching. This is an important point, and will apply to all embroidery projects.

There are two parts to an embroidery hoop. To separate the parts, loosen the screw slightly on the outer ring and pull out the inner ring gently. Place the tear-away backing, then the fabric over the inner ring (the sketch of your dog should be in the centre). I also recommend sticking the water-soluble stabiliser with the transfer on top of the fabric (see page 20). Push down the outer ring around the outside to secure the fabric, making sure the fabric is taut.

If using a stretchy fabric (e.g. a T-shirt), it is vital to use a tear-away stabiliser and ensure the fabric is not over-stretched. The stretchy fabric of the T-shirt should sit naturally flat on top of the backing.

Tighten the screw on the outer ring or gently pull the fabric outside of the hoop to avoid any wrinkles or puckers on the fabric. Try to hold the ring while pulling fabric on the outside of the hoop to ensure the rings don't separate. The fabric inside of the hoop should feel like a drum with a little bounce to it.

Stitch Textures

Straight stitch

You can create some amazing textures by using only the straight stitch setting on your sewing machine. It is very useful for filling in areas and shading, and can also be used for 'writing'.

The stitch length is determined by how fast you move the hoop while sewing. It really does not matter how long the stitch length is, but keep moving the hoop in a constant speed and you will get neat stitches of a similar length.

To fill sections with straight stitch, all you have to do is simply start from one side of the section, stitch in a straight line until you reach the other side, then stitch back to the side you started with. Work your way across the section slowly. To create the density of the embroidery, stitch over the same area a few times until you are happy with the look.

Zigzag stitch

This is ideal for filling in large areas, and is also great for creating a fur-like appearance.

To create zigzag stitches, move the hoop backwards and forwards while stitching. Using this motion, fill in sections from one side to another. Be gentle and move slowly so you do not snap the needle, which can happen if the movement is too fast and aggressive. As with straight stitch, it is best to work at a constant speed, and you can layer up stitches to create density, if you wish.

Feel free to experiment with other types of stitching for different effects. Freehand/free-motion embroidery is ultimately sketching with your sewing machine needle, so there is no limit to what you can do.

Embroidery Tips & Tricks

These handy suggestions will help to eliminate the most common problems when creating freehand or free-motion embroidery. They often include thread and needle breakages, as well as avoiding bobbin threads pulling through, causing small loops appearing.

ONE

•

A clean sewing machine is always a good start

Each time you use your machine, make sure there are no loose threads or lint causing it to catch.

TWO

•

Check the machine is threaded correctly

Missing one small thread guide loop can cause the needle and thread to break when stitching. All machines have slightly different thread guides (these are various loops that you run the thread through before looping it into the needle, keeping the thread from getting tangled and distributing the tension evenly). Thread guide instructions are often marked clearly on the machine or in the manual. If necessary, re-thread the top and bobbin thread to make sure it is done correctly.

THREE

•

Check tension and adjust if needed

Tension is what keeps the top and bobbin thread in equal tension with one another. If the tension is not right, it causes stitches to be uneven. To test the tension of the machine, run a couple of seams on a spare piece of fabric. If the thread is too tight, causing the fabric to bunch together or too loose and falling apart, this means you have an issue with the tension. You can adjust the tension by turning the tension dial. Be very careful and only turn the dial gently as it often only takes a very small adjustment to fix the problem.

FIVE

•

Practice makes perfect

Get comfortable with moving the embroidery hoop around your machine. Everyone has a slightly different technique when stitching, so work out a way to move the hoop with ease. Also, try out different stitches on different fabrics until you feel confident.

SIX

•

Always remember to have fun

Embroidery is meant to be therapeutic, so don't stress too much about making it perfect. Little imperfections can make your embroidery unique and special.

FOUR

•

Make sure the needle is sharp

A blunt needle can easily snag and make holes in the fabric while stitching. Change the needle after each project to avoid the hassle.

The
Projects

The translation of the word beagle in French is 'loudmouth' –
take from that what you will.

The world's most famous beagle is Snoopy.

MATERIALS

Beagle template   (see page 138)

Baseball cap

Spare piece of non-stretch fabric -
    pre-shrunk cotton or linen
    works best

EQUIPMENT

Sewing machine with free-motion/
    darning foot

Size 70/80 needle

Embroidery bobbin thread

Marker pen

Heat and bond ultra iron-on adhesive

12-cm (5-in) embroidery hoop

Embroidery scissors

Hand-sewing needle (optional)

EMBROIDERY THREAD

① #1527 light tan,
    approximately 2.25 m (2.5 yards)

② #1057 mid tan,
    approximately 2.6 m (2.8 yards)

③ #1257 dark tan,
    approximately 1.3 m (1.4 yards)

④ #1001 white,
    approximately 8.4 m (9.2 yards)

⑤ #1086 off white,
    approximately 1.6 m (1.7 yards)

⑥ #1053 blush,
    approximately 1 m (1 yard)

⑦ #1058 hazel brown,
    approximately 1 m (1 yard)

⑧ #1000 black,
    approximately 75 cm (0.6 yards)

STITCH TECHNIQUES

Straight stitch   (see page 33)

1. Trace the template on to the fabric (see page 26). Iron on the adhesive to the back of the fabric and secure centrally in the embroidery hoop. For this project, it is best to embroider onto fabric first (similar to making a patch), then iron the patch onto the baseball cap.

2. Stitch all sections marked ① with thread #1527 light tan, then the sections marked ② with thread #1057 mid tan, and then sections marked ③ with thread #1257 dark tan, all using straight stitch.

3. Stitch all sections marked ④ with thread #1001 white, then all sections marked ⑤ with thread #1086 off white using straight stitch. I find it is always easiest to start with the largest sections and work in towards the smaller ones.

4. Straight stitch the nose section marked ⑥ with thread #1053 blush. Then complete the rest of the nose and eye sections marked ⑦ with thread #1058 hazel brown with straight stitch.

5. Finally, stitch sections marked ⑧ with thread #1000 black, using straight stitch.

6. Once finished, remove the fabric from the embroidery hoop and peel off the paper backing of the adhesive. Carefully cut around the embroidery, making sure you only cut the fabric and not any embroidery threads as this will cause the embroidery to unravel.

7. Place the patch onto the front of the baseball cap and use a hot iron to make the patch to stick. If you wish, you could also use a hand-sewing needle, loosely stitching around the patch with clear thread. Embroidery bobbin thread is ideal for this as it is not only clear, but also very strong.

2

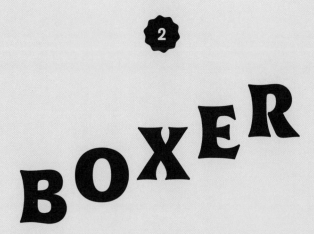

Supposedly, the boxer is named so because of its similarity to a boxer in the ring when it plays – standing on hind legs, front paws in the air.

The boxer also is believed to have the longest tongue of all dogs.

MATERIALS

Boxer template   (see page 139)

Add-on embroideries   (see page 134)

Denim jacket

EQUIPMENT

Sewing machine with free-motion/
   darning foot

Size 80/90 needle

Embroidery bobbin thread

Marker pen

Water-soluble stabiliser,
   such as Sticky Fabri-Solvy

30.5-cm (12-in) embroidery hoop

Embroidery scissors

EMBROIDERY THREAD

① #1527 light tan,
   approximately 37 m (40 yards)

② #1057 mid tan,
   approximately 30 m (33 yards)

③ #1158 deep brown,
   approximately 18.5 m (20.2 yards)

④ #1241 charcoal,
   approximately 3.8 m (4.2 yards)

⑤ #1000 black,
   approximately 1.8 m (2 yards)

⑥ #1058 hazel brown,
   approximately 1.6 m (1.75 yards)

⑦ #1001 white,
   approximately 4.4 m (4.8 yards)

STITCH TECHNIQUES

Straight stitch   (see page 33)

1. Trace the template on to water-soluble stabiliser (see page 26) and stick onto the middle back of the denim jacket. Secure centrally in the embroidery hoop.

2. Stitch all sections marked ① with thread #1527 light tan, all sections marked ② with thread #1057 mid tan and all sections marked ③ with thread #1158 deep brown, all using straight stitch.

3. Stitch all sections ④ with thread #1241 charcoal, then all sections marked ⑤ with thread #1000 black using straight stitch.

4. Straight stitch the eye sections marked ⑥ with thread #1058 hazel brown.

5. Use thread #1001 white to straight stitch sections marked ⑦ and your embroidery is finished.

6. To make this embroidery even more fun, I have added a few embroidered bones around the boxer. Please see add-on embroideries (page 134) for template and thread colours.

7. Once finished, remove from the embroidery hoop. Rinse off the stabiliser with lukewarm water and hang to dry naturally. Give the denim jacket a good press and steam to remove any creases.

3

BOSTON TERRIER

Boston terriers are often referred to as 'the American gentleman'
because of their dapper, tuxedo-like appearance.

The breed was so beloved in its hometown that it was named
the state dog of Massachusetts in 1970.

MATERIALS

Boston terrier template (see page 140)

White collared shirt

EQUIPMENT

Sewing machine with free-motion/
    darning foot

Size 70/80 needle

Embroidery bobbin thread

Marker pen

Water-soluble stabiliser,
    such as Sticky Fabri-Solvy

Tear-away stabiliser

12-cm (5-in) embroidery hoop

Embroidery scissors

EMBROIDERY THREAD

① #1001 white,
    approximately 5.6 m (6.1 yards)

② #1086 off white,
    approximately 2 m (2.2 yards)

③ #1241 charcoal,
    approximately 13.25 m (14.5 yards)

④ #1000 black,
    approximately 10 m (11 yards)

⑤ #1058 hazel brown,
    approximately 1.6 m (1.7 yards)

STITCH TECHNIQUES

Straight stitch   (see page 33)

1. Trace the template onto water-soluble stabiliser (see page 26) and stick to the collar. Then attach the embroidery hoop and the tear-away stabiliser. It is up to you which side of the collar you wish to start on.

2. Stitch all sections marked ① with thread #1001 white, then the sections marked ② with thread #1086 off white, using straight stitch.

3. Straight stitch all sections marked ③ with thread #1241 charcoal, then all sections marked ④ with thread #1000 black.

4. Lastly, use thread #1058 hazel brown to straight stitch the eye sections marked ⑤.

5. Remove the hoop and tear or rinse off the stabilisers. Repeat the steps above on the other collar tip, making sure the positioning matches on both sides.

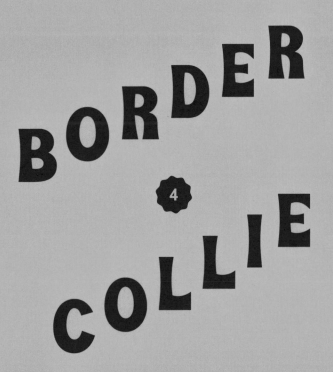

BORDER

4

COLLIE

The border collie is a very fast learner, and will get to grips
with new tricks and commands after a couple of tries.

A border collie called Chaser was crowned the world's most intelligent
dog after it was established that she could recognise
the names of more than 1,000 objects.

MATERIALS

Border collie template (see page 141)

Add-on embroideries   (see page 134)

Cushion cover, 45 x 45 cm (18 x 18 in)

EQUIPMENT

Sewing machine with free-motion/
    darning foot

Size 80/90 needle

Embroidery bobbin thread

Marker pen

Water-soluble stabiliser,
    such as Sticky Fabri-Solvy

30.5-cm (12-in) embroidery hoop

Embroidery scissors

EMBROIDERY THREAD

① #1000 black,
    approximately 35 m (38 yards)

② #1241 charcoal,
    approximately 25 m (27 yards)

③ #1361 dark grey,
    approximately 37 m (40 yards)

④ #1001 white,
    approximately 20 m (22 yards)

⑤ #1321 pink,
    approximately 1.6 m (1.75 yards)

⑥ #1858 dark brown,
    approximately 2.5 m (2.7 yards)

STITCH TECHNIQUES

Straight stitch   (see page 33)

Zigzag stitch   (see page 33)

1. Transfer the template to one side of the cushion cover (see page 26). I recommend tracing on to water-soluble stabiliser, and securing centrally in the embroidery hoop. Be careful when you start stitching that you don't accidentally embroider both sides of the cushion cover together.

2. Stitch all sections marked ① with thread #1000 black, using straight stitch. Start with the largest area and work your way down to the smaller sections.

3. Stitch all sections marked ② with thread #1241 charcoal. Use zigzag stitch except for the nose, which uses straight stitch.

4. Stitch all sections marked ③ with thread #1361 dark grey, using zigzag stitch.

5. Stitch all sections marked ④ with thread #1001 white, using straight stitch.

6. Stitch all sections marked ⑤ with thread #1321 pink, using straight stitch.

7. Stitch the eyes section marked ⑥ with thread #1858 dark brown, using straight stitch.

8. I have added a few red floating love hearts to this design – have a look at the extra add-on embroideries section (page 134) for templates and thread colour. Feel free to incorporate any extra add-on embroidery to the projects.

9. Once you have completed stitching, rinse off the water-soluble stabiliser with lukewarm water and let it dry naturally.

5

GOLDEN RETRIEVER

Golden retrievers are big fans of water – you'll often find them
following their ball into rivers, lakes and seas.

Golden retrievers are known to be one of the friendliest breeds,
even when it comes to cats.

MATERIALS

Golden retriever
    template   (see page 142)

Navy sweater

EQUIPMENT

Sewing machine with free-motion/
    darning foot

Size 70/80 ballpoint needle

Embroidery bobbin thread

Marker pen

Water-soluble stabiliser,
    such as Sticky Fabri-Solvy

Tear-away stabiliser

30.5-cm (12-in) embroidery hoop

Embroidery scissors

EMBROIDERY THREAD

① #1084 light gold,
    approximately 48 m (52 yards)

② #1055 mid gold,
    approximately 35 m (38 yards)

③ #1256 dark gold,
    approximately 24 m (26 yards)

④ #1321 pink,
    approximately 7.3 m (8 yards)

⑤ #1241 charcoal,
    approximately 7 m (7.7 yards)

⑥ #1058 hazel brown,
    approximately 1.4 m (1.5 yards)

⑦ #1000 black,
    approximately 5.3 m (5.7 yards)

⑧ #1001 white,
    approximately 1.2 m (1.3 yards)

STITCH TECHNIQUES

Straight stitch   (see page 33)

1. Trace the template on to water-soluble stabiliser (see page 26) and attach to the middle of the front of the sweater. Use tear-away stabiliser on the inside of the sweater and secure all three layers in the embroidery hoop.

2. Stitch all sections marked ① with thread #1084 light gold, using straight stitch.

3. Straight stitch all sections marked ② with thread #1055 mid gold and all sections marked ③ with thread #1256 dark gold.

4. Use straight stitch to complete the tongue section marked ④ with thread #1321 pink, then the nose section marked ⑤ with thread #1241 charcoal and the eye sections marked ⑥ with thread #1058 hazel brown.

5. Fill in the sections marked ⑦ with thread #1000 black, using straight stitch.

6. Lastly, fill in the small sections marked ⑧ – eyes and teeth – with thread #1001 white, using straight stitch.

7. When the embroidery is completed, unscrew the embroidery hoop. Tear off the tear-away stabiliser and rinse off the water-soluble stabiliser with lukewarm water.

BULL TERRIER

The bull terrier's most distinguishing feature
is its triangle-shaped eyes.

Bull terriers are big and muscular, but this belies
their sweet and caring nature.

MATERIALS

Bull terrier template (see page 143)

Add-on embroideries   (see page 134)

Striped T-shirt (wash and iron
    before embroidering, in case
    of shrinkage)

EQUIPMENT

Sewing machine with free-motion/
    darning foot

Size 60/70 ballpoint needle

Embroidery bobbin thread

Water-soluble stabiliser,
    such as Sticky Fabri-Solvy

Tear-away stabiliser

30.5-cm (12-in) embroidery hoop

Embroidery scissors

EMBROIDERY THREAD

① #1001 white,
    approximately 78 m (85 yards)

② #1086 off white,
    approximately 30 m (32 yards)

③ #1053 pale pink,
    approximately 12 m (13 yards)

④ #1054 dark pink,
    approximately 7 m (7.7 yards)

⑤ #1241 charcoal,
    approximately 6.6 m (7.2 yards)

⑥ #1000 black,
    approximately 4.5 m (4.9 yards)

STITCH TECHNIQUES

Straight stitch   (see page 33)

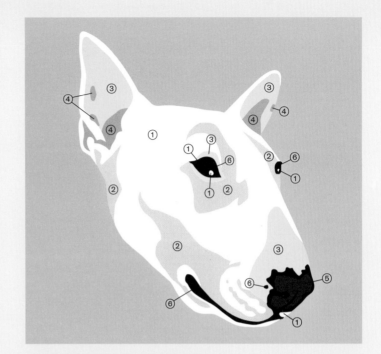

1. T-shirt fabric is thin and stretchy, so using both stabilisers is a good idea. Transfer the template onto the water-soluble stabiliser (see page 26) and stick on the outer side of T-shirt. Place the tear-away stabiliser on the inside of T-shirt and secure all layers in the embroidery hoop (see page 32).

2. Stitch all sections marked ① with thread #1001 white, then all sections marked ② with thread #1086 off white, using straight stitch.

3. Next, straight stitch all sections marked ③ with thread #1053 pale pink, follow by all sections marked ④ with thread #1054 dark pink.

4. Stitch the nose section marked ⑤ with thread #1241 charcoal, using straight stitch.

5. Lastly, use thread #1000 black to straight stitch sections marked ⑥.

6. I have added a few red floating love hearts to this design – have a look at the extra add-on embroideries section (page 134) for templates and thread colour. Feel free to incorporate any extra add-on embroidery to the projects.

7. Remove the tear-away stabiliser with caution, as T-shirt fabric rips easily. Rinse off the water-soluble stabiliser with lukewarm water. Allow to dry, then iron the T-shirt.

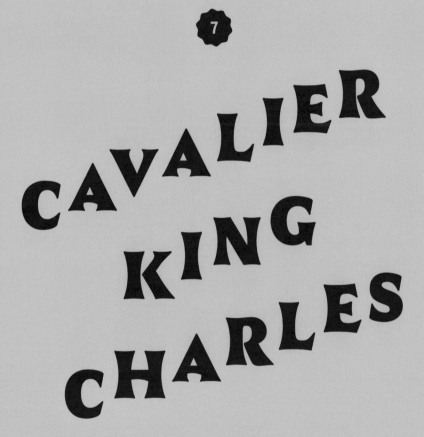

Unsurprisingly, this breed was named after King Charles II,
such was his love of these dogs.

They often had a purpose beyond their status as best friend material.
Known as 'comfort' dogs, their owners would keep them in their beds,
so that fleas bit the dogs instead, to avoid catching deadly diseases.

MATERIALS

Cavalier King
   Charles template   (see page 144)

Green T-shirt (wash and iron
   before embroidering, in case
   of shrinkage)

EQUIPMENT

Sewing machine with free-motion/
   darning foot

Size 60/70 ballpoint needle

Embroidery bobbin thread

Water-soluble stabiliser,
   such as Sticky Fabri-Solvy

Tear-away stabiliser

30.5-cm (12-in) embroidery hoop

Embroidery scissors

EMBROIDERY THREAD

① #1001 white,
   approximately 2.2 m (2.4 yards)

② #1086 off white,
   approximately 9 m (9.8 yards)

③ #1173 golden amber,
   approximately 40 m (44 yards)

④ #1057 mid tan,
   approximately 34 m (37 yards)

⑤ #1258 dark amber,
   approximately 30 m (32 yards)

⑥ #1129 deep brown,
   approximately 15 m (16.4 yards)

⑦ #1000 black,
   approximately 3 m (3.2 yards)

STITCH TECHNIQUES

Straight stitch   (see page 33)

Zigzag stitch   (see page 33)

1. Transfer the template onto water-soluble stabiliser with marker pen (see page 26). Place on top of the T-shirt with the tear-away stabiliser underneath. Secure centrally in the embroidery hoop.

2. Straight stitch all sections marked ① with thread #1001 white, then all sections marked ② with thread #1086 off white.

3. Complete sections marked ③ with thread #1173 golden amber, sections marked ④ with thread #1057 mid tan and sections marked ⑤ with thread #1258 dark amber, all using zigzag stitch to create texture.

4. Use thread #1129 deep brown to straight stitch sections marked ⑥ and thread #1000 black to straight stitch sections marked ⑦.

5. Tear or rinse off the stabilisers and let the T-shirt dry. The T-shirt will have creases so give it a good press with a steam iron before wearing.

8

Chihuahuas are known to be beloved among celebrities
such as Paris Hilton, Ashton Kutcher, Madonna, Marilyn Monroe,
Sandra Bullock and Scarlett Johansson.

Chihuahuas first found global fame in a series of Taco Bell
advertisements in the 1990s.

MATERIALS

Chihuahua template   (see page 145)

Add-on embroideries   (see page 134)

Striped tote bag, approximately
    43 x 46 cm (17 x 18 in)

EQUIPMENT

Sewing machine with free-motion/
    darning foot

Size 80/90 needle

Embroidery bobbin thread

Marker pen

Water-soluble stabiliser,
    such as Sticky Fabri-Solvy

30.5-cm (12-in) embroidery hoop

Embroidery scissors

EMBROIDERY THREAD

① #1001 white,
   approximately 75 m (82 yards)

② #1086 off white,
   approximately 18 m (19.6 yards)

③ #1241 charcoal,
   approximately 12 m (13 yards)

④ #1000 black,
   approximately 30 m (33 yards)

⑤ #1138 golden tan,
   approximately 32 m (35 yards)

⑥ #1257 dark tan,
   approximately 15 m (16.4 yards)

⑦ #1058 dark brown,
   approximately 3 m (3.3 yards)

STITCH TECHNIQUES

Straight stitch   (see page 33)

Zigzag stitch   (see page 33)

1. Trace the template onto the water-soluble stabiliser (see page 26) and stick on the front of the tote bag. Then stretch the bag on the embroidery hoop, taking care not to enclose the other side of the tote bag as you don't want to stitch through both sides of the bag.

2. Stitch all sections marked ① with thread #1001 white, using straight stitch, starting with the largest area and working your way down to the smaller sections. Fill all the white sections ① on both chihuahuas.

3. Stitch all sections marked ② with thread #1086 off white, using straight stitch.

4. Straight stitch all sections marked ③ with thread #1241 charcoal and all sections marked ④ with thread #1000 black.

5. Use zigzag stitch to fill in all sections marked ⑤ with thread #1138 golden tan and all sections marked ⑥ with thread #1257 dark tan.

6. Straight stitch the eye sections marked ⑦ with thread #1058 dark brown.

7. Use straight stitch to stitch all sections of the extra red and pink heart embroidery (see page 134 for the add-on embroideries templates and thread colours).

8. Once you have completed stitching, rinse off the water-soluble stabiliser with lukewarm water and let the bag dry naturally.

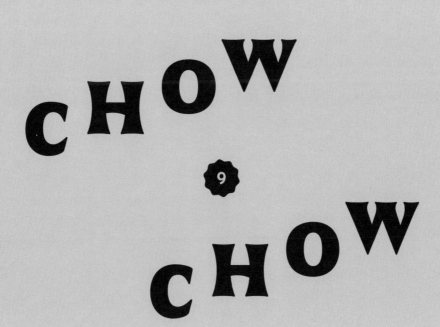

CHOW
9
CHOW

Chow chows are one of the oldest known breeds,
supposedly having existed for 2,000–3,000 years.

Chow chows have very unique coloured purple tongues, which turn
much darker with age. Older dogs' tongues are almost blue-black.

MATERIALS

Chow chow template   (see page 146)

Child's jacket
  (a thin fabric works best)

EQUIPMENT

Sewing machine with free-motion/
  darning foot

Size 60/70 ballpoint needle

Embroidery bobbin thread

Tear-away stabiliser

25.5-cm (10-in) embroidery hoop

Embroidery scissors

EMBROIDERY THREAD

① #1527 light tan,
   approximately 97 m (106 yards)

② #1057 mid tan,
   approximately 70 m (76.5 yards)

③ #1257 dark tan,
   approximately 27 m (29.5 yards)

④ #1080 lilac,
   approximately 9 m (9.8 yards)

⑤ #1129 deep brown,
   approximately 3.2 m (3.5 yards)

⑥ #1000 black,
   approximately 17 m (18.5 yards)

⑦ #1001 white,
   approximately 1.5 m (1.6 yards)

STITCH TECHNIQUES

Straight stitch   (see page 33)

1. The template can be traced straight onto the jacket (see page 26). Place the tear-away stabiliser underneath the traced design and secure in the embroidery hoop.

2. Straight stitch all sections marked ① with thread #1527 light tan, all sections marked ② with thread #1057 mid tan and all sections marked ③ with #1257 dark tan.

3. Using thread #1080 lilac, straight stitch the tongue section marked ④, then use thread #1129 deep brown for the nose section marked ⑤.

4. Straight stitch all sections marked ⑥ with thread #1000 black and sections marked ⑦ with thread #1001 white.

5. Remove the tear-away stabiliser and carefully iron around the embroidery to get rid of any creases.

10

What came first, the sausage or the dog? The dog, as the sausage was named in honour of the dachshund.

The dachshund was the first Olympic mascot.

MATERIALS

Dachshund template   (see page 147)

Non-stretch knitted scarf,
    minimum 20 cm (8 in) wide

EQUIPMENT

Sewing machine with free-motion/
    darning foot

Size 70/80 ballpoint needle

Embroidery bobbin thread

Water-soluble stabiliser,
    such as Sticky Fabri-Solvy

Tear-away stabiliser

15-cm (6-in) embroidery hoop

Embroidery scissors

EMBROIDERY THREAD

① #1527 light tan,
    approximately 12 m (13 yards)

② #1258 dark amber,
    approximately 16 m (17.5 yards)

③ #1158 deep brown,
    approximately 10 m (11 yards)

④ #1858 dark brown,
    approximately 2.5 m (2.7 yards)

⑤ #1000 black,
    approximately 2 m (2.2 yards)

⑥ #1001 white,
    approximately 1 m (1 yard)

STITCH TECHNIQUES

Straight stitch   (see page 33)

1. Decide where you would like to position your embroidery. I normally have the embroidery on the left-hand side of the scarf, but this is just a personal preference.

2. With knitted fabrics, it is best to use both water-soluble stabiliser and tear-away stabiliser. Trace the template onto the water-soluble stabiliser (see page 26) and stick to the upper side of scarf. Place the tear-away stabiliser on the underside. Secure the scarf in the embroidery hoop, making sure the scarf is flat but not stretched.

3. Stitch all sections marked ① with thread #1527 light tan, using straight stitch.

4. Stitch all sections marked ② with thread #1258 dark amber, then all sections marked ③ with thread #1158 deep brown, using straight stitch.

5. Stitch the eyes and nose sections marked ④ with thread #1858 dark brown, using straight stitch.

6. Stitch all sections marked ⑤ with thread #1000 black, using straight stitch.

7. Stitch all sections marked ⑥ with thread #1001 white, using straight stitch.

8. Once you have completed the embroidery, rinse away the water-soluble stabiliser with lukewarm water and tear off the tear-away stabiliser.

Dalmatians were often affectionately referred to as 'Spotted Dicks',
like the old-fashioned English sponge pudding.

All Dalmatian puppies are born white – their spots appear
when they are around four weeks old.

MATERIALS

Dalmatian template   (see page 148)

Long smock dress

EQUIPMENT

Sewing machine with free-motion/
  darning foot

Size 80/90 needle

Embroidery bobbin thread

Marker pen

Water-soluble stabiliser,
  such as Sticky Fabri-Solvy

30.5-cm (12-in) embroidery hoop

Embroidery scissors

EMBROIDERY THREAD

① #1001 white,
  approximately 80 m (87 yards)

② #1086 off white,
  approximately 12 m (13 yards)

③ #1361 dark grey,
  approximately 18 m (19.7 yards)

④ #1000 black,
  approximately 29 m (32 yards)

⑤ #1858 dark brown,
  approximately 1 m (1 yard)

⑥ #1027 sky blue,
  approximately 1 m (1 yard)

STITCH TECHNIQUES

Straight stitch   (see page 33)

1. Transfer the template onto the water-soluble stabiliser (see page 26) and stick to the dress, then secure in the embroidery hoop.

2. Stitch all sections marked ① with thread #1001 white using straight stitch, then all sections marked ② with thread #1086 off white, also using straight stitch.

3. Straight stitch all sections marked ③ with thread #1361 dark grey.

4. Stitch all sections marked ④ with thread #1000 black, using straight stitch. There are a lot of small dotted areas to straight stitch, so take your time and remember it is not the end of the world if you stitch slightly outside the marked areas.

5. Stitch the eye section marked ⑤ with thread #1858 dark brown and the other eye section marked ⑥ with thread #1027 sky blue, using straight stitch. This gorgeous pup happens to have eyes of different colours. You can, of course, use one colour for both eyes if you wish.

6. Rinse away the water-soluble stabiliser with lukewarm water and hang up the dress to dry naturally. Once dry, give the embroidery a quick iron.

FRENCH

12

BULLDOG

Unlike other breeds, Frenchies are not fantastic swimmers,
mainly down to their heavy, squat frame.

French bulldogs aren't ones for barking, but that doesn't mean
they are quiet – they have a complex system of yawns, yips
and gargles to get attention and express themselves.

MATERIALS

French bulldog template (see page 149)

Pink sweatshirt

EQUIPMENT

Sewing machine with free-motion/
    darning foot

Size 60/70 ballpoint needle

Embroidery bobbin thread

Tear-away stabiliser

Water-soluble stabiliser,
    such as Sticky Fabri-Solvy

30.5-cm (12-in) embroidery hoop

Embroidery scissors

EMBROIDERY THREAD

① #1118 light blue,
    approximately 34 m (37 yards)

② #1461 blue,
    approximately 27 m (29.5 yards)

③ #1164 dark blue,
    approximately 38 m (41.5 yards)

④ #1321 pink,
    approximately 1.6 m (1.7 yards)

⑤ #1058 hazel brown,
    approximately 1.6 m (1.7 yards)

⑥ #1001 white,
    approximately 16 m (17 yards)

⑦ #1000 black,
    approximately 1 m (1 yard)

STITCH TECHNIQUES

Straight stitch   (see page 33)

INSTRUCTIONS

1. Transfer the template on to the water-soluble stabiliser, then stick to the outside of the sweatshirt (see page 26). Apply the tear-away stabiliser to the inside of the sweatshirt and secure all layers centrally in the embroidery hoop.

2. Straight stitch all sections marked ① with thread #1118 light blue, all sections marked ② with thread #1461 blue and all sections marked ③ with thread #1164 dark blue. Start with the largest sections and work down to the smaller ones.

3. Stitch the tongue section marked ④ with thread #1321 pink and the eye sections marked ⑤ with thread #1058 hazel brown, using straight stitch.

4. Use thread #1001 white to straight stitch all sections marked ⑥ and thread #1000 black to straight stitch outline sections marked ⑦.

5. Tear or rinse off the stabilisers. Press with a steam iron.

13

PUG

A group of three or more of these dogs is known as a grumble of pugs.

Pugs are know for their charming and loveable demeanor,
as well as having a high level of sass.

MATERIALS

Pug template   (see page 150)

Bomber jacket

EQUIPMENT

Sewing machine with free-motion/
   darning foot

Size 80/90 needle

Embroidery bobbin thread

Marker pen

Water-soluble stabiliser,
   such as Sticky Fabri-Solvy

30.5-cm (12-in) embroidery hoop

Embroidery scissors

EMBROIDERY THREAD

① #1082 beige,
   approximately 44 m (48 yards)

② #1126 dark beige,
   approximately 22 m (24 yards)

③ #1241 charcoal,
   approximately 34 m (37 yards)

④ #1361 light grey,
   approximately 26 m (28 yards)

⑤ #1053 blush,
   approximately 1.4 m (1.5 yards)

⑥ #1000 black,
   approximately 40 m (44 yards)

⑦ #1058 hazel brown,
   approximately 2.6 m (2.8 yards)

⑧ #1001 white,
   approximately 2.25 m (2.8 yards)

STITCH TECHNIQUES

Straight stitch   (see page 33)

1. Trace the pug template onto the water-soluble stabiliser (see page 26) and stick to the back of the bomber jacket. Unzip the jacket and secure centrally in the embroidery hoop. Make sure the front of the jacket and sleeves do not get caught while stitching.

2. Stitch all sections marked ① with thread #1082 beige and all sections marked ② with thread #1126 dark beige, using straight stitch.

3. Use straight stitch on all sections marked ③ with thread #1241 charcoal and sections marked ④ with thread #1361 light grey.

4. Stitch that little pink nose section marked ⑤ with thread #1053 blush, using straight stitch.

5. Straight stitch all sections marked ⑥ with thread #1000 black. Be careful as some of the sections are very narrow, so work slowly.

6. Stitch all sections marked ⑦ with thread #1058 hazel brown and all sections marked ⑧ with thread #1001 white.

7. When the embroidery is finished, rinse off the water-soluble stabiliser with lukewarm water. Hang up the jacket to dry naturally, then press with a steam iron if necessary.

Skill Level • Easy

Finished Size
7 x 13 cm (2¾ x 5 in)

Time • 3–4 hours

14

HUSKY

Huskies might look like they are good guard dogs, but their sweet, friendly nature means that couldn't be further from the truth.

Huskies are known as very efficient escapees, digging under fences and pulling off their leads (leashes).

MATERIALS

Husky template   (see page 151)

Bandana

EQUIPMENT

Sewing machine with free-motion/
    darning foot

Size 70/80 needle

Embroidery bobbin thread

Marker pen

Tear-away stabiliser

12-cm (5-in) embroidery hoop

Embroidery scissors

EMBROIDERY THREAD

① #1000 black,
    approximately 12 m (13 yards)

② #1241 charcoal,
    approximately 8 m (8.7 yards)

③ #1001 white,
    approximately 20 m (22 yards)

④ #1086 off white,
    approximately 8.5 m (9.3 yards)

⑤ #1057 rosewood,
    approximately 2 m (2.2 yards)

⑥ #1027 sky blue,
    approximately 1 m (1 yard)

STITCH TECHNIQUES

Straight stitch   (see page 33)

Zigzag stitch   (see page 33)

1. Transfer the template on to one corner of the bandana (see page 26). Add a layer of tear-away stabiliser and secure centrally in the embroidery hoop.

2. Using straight stitch, stitch all sections marked ① with thread #1000 black and all sections marked ② with thread #1241 charcoal.

3. Use thread #1001 white to straight stitch all sections marked ③ and thread #1086 off white to zigzag stitch all sections marked ④.

4. Straight stitch the inner ear sections marked ⑤ with thread #1057 rosewood.

5. Straight stitch the eye sections marked ⑥ with thread #1027 sky blue.

6. Once finished, remove the fabric from the embroidery hoop, tear away the stabiliser and iron flat.

ENGLISH

15

BULLDOG

English bulldogs have a calm, courageous and friendly personality,
making them one of the most popular dog breeds in the UK.

They are great for city dwellers as they do not require
a great deal of exercise.

MATERIALS

English bulldog
    template   (see page 152)

Blue workwear jacket

EQUIPMENT

Sewing machine with free-motion/
    darning foot

Size 70/80 needle

Embroidery bobbin thread

Marker pen

Tear-away stabiliser

35.5-cm (14-in) embroidery hoop

Embroidery scissors

EMBROIDERY THREAD

① #1001 white,
approximately 100 m (109 yards)

② #1086 off white,
approximately 40 m (43 yards)

③ #1255 light sand,
approximately 27 m (29.5 yards)

④ #1057 mid tan,
approximately 24 m (26 yards)

⑤ #1256 dark gold,
approximately 15 m (16.5 yards)

⑥ #1321 pink,
approximately 4 m (4.3 yards)

⑦ #1241 charcoal,
approximately 11 m (12 yards)

⑧ #1058 hazel brown,
approximately 1.7 m (1.9 yards)

⑨ #1000 black,
approximately 22 m (24 yards)

STITCH TECHNIQUES

Straight stitch   (see page 33)

1. Centre the template on the back of the jacket and trace (see page 26). Place the tear-away stabiliser inside the jacket and stretch the embroidery hoop over the back, making sure the template is in the middle of the hoop.

2. Stitch all sections marked ① with thread #1001 white and all sections marked ② with thread #1086 off white, using straight stitch.

3. Use thread #1255 light sand to straight stitch all sections marked ③, thread #1057 mid tan for all sections marked ④ and thread #1256 dark gold for all sections marked ⑤.

4. The tongue section marked ⑥ is stitched with thread #1321 pink, using straight stitch.

5. Stitch all sections marked ⑦ with thread #1241 charcoal and all sections marked ⑧ with thread #1058 hazel brown, again using straight stitch.

6. Now use thread #1000 black to straight stitch the remaining sections ⑨.

7. Remove the embroidery hoop once the embroidery is finished and tear away the stabiliser, then iron the jacket.

16

LABRADOR

Labradors are often known for their appetites,
which are borderline unstoppable.

In 1925, after killing the cat belonging to US Governor Gifford
Pinchot's wife, a black Labrador retriever named Pep was sentenced
to life in jail without parole.

MATERIALS

Labrador template   (see page 153)

Straw hat

Spare piece of non-stretch fabric - pre-shrunk white cotton or linen works best

EQUIPMENT

Sewing machine with free-motion/ darning foot

Size 60/70 ballpoint needle

Embroidery bobbin thread

Marker pen

Heat and bond ultra iron-on adhesive

10 cm (10 in) embroidery hoop

Embroidery scissors

Hand-sewing needle (optional)

EMBROIDERY THREAD

① #1058 hazel brown, approximately 13 m (14 yards)

② #1145 chocolate, approximately 16 m (17.5 yards)

③ #1059 dark chocolate, approximately 10 m (11 yards)

④ #1425 yellow, approximately 1 m (1 yard)

⑤ #1000 black, approximately 1 m (1 yard)

⑥ #1001 white, approximately 1 m (1 yard)

STITCH TECHNIQUES

Straight stitch   (see page 33)

1. I recommend embroidering on a piece of fabric first and attaching that to the straw hat (it would be too fiddly to move the straw hat around the sewing machine). Transfer the template to the fabric (see page 26) and iron on the adhesive, then secure in the embroidery hoop.

2. Straight stitch all sections marked ① with thread #1058 hazel brown, all sections marked ② with thread #1145 chocolate and all sections marked ③ with thread #1059 dark chocolate.

3. Straight stitch in the eye sections marked ④ with thread #1425 yellow.

4. Use thread #1000 black to straight stitch all sections marked ⑤ and thread #1001 white to straight stitch both eye sections marked ⑥.

5. Remove the paper backing and cut around the embroidery carefully, being sure not to catch any embroidery threads.

6. Using a very hot iron, press the embroidery patch onto the straw hat. Also hand stitch the embroidery in place with clear thread if you wish – this is optional as the adhesive should have enough hold.

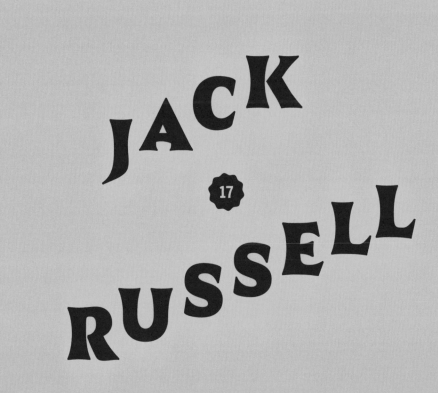

Although Jack Russells are diminutive in stature,
they can jump up to 1.5 m (5 ft) in the air.

Jack Russells are often the life and soul of a party,
wanting to be everyone's friend.

MATERIALS

Jack Russell template (see page 154)

Cushion cover, 45 x 45 cm (18 x 18 in)

EQUIPMENT

Sewing machine with free-motion/
  darning foot

Size 70/80 needle

Embroidery bobbin thread

Marker pen

Tear-away stabiliser

30.5-cm (12-in) embroidery hoop

Embroidery scissors

EMBROIDERY THREAD

① #1527 light tan,
  approximately 44 m (48 yards)

② #1057 mid tan,
  approximately 52 m (57 yards)

③ #1258 dark amber,
  approximately 11 m (12 yards)

④ #1053 blush,
  approximately 6.6 m (7.2 yards)

⑤ #1086 off white,
  approximately 6.6 m (7.2 yards)

⑥ #1241 charcoal,
  approximately 6.5 m (7.1 yards)

⑦ #1001 white,
  approximately 26 m (28 yards)

⑧ #1000 black,
  approximately 6 m (6.6 yards)

STITCH TECHNIQUES

Straight stitch   (see page 33)

1. Put the template inside the cushion cover and trace onto one side of the cover only (see page 26).

2. Place the tear-away stabiliser inside the cushion cover and stretch the embroidery hoop over the side of the cushion cover with the template on. Be careful not to stitch through both sides of the cover.

3. Stitch all sections marked ① with thread #1527 light tan, all sections marked ② with thread #1057 mid tan and all sections marked ③ with thread #1258 dark amber, using straight stitch.

4. Stitch the ear sections marked ④ with thread #1053 blush, using straight stitch.

5. Straight stitch all sections marked ⑤ with thread #1086 off white, then the nose section marked ⑥ with thread #1241 charcoal.

6. Stitch all sections marked ⑦ with thread #1001 white and all sections marked ⑧ with thread #1000 black, using straight stitch.

7. Remove the embroidery hoop once the embroidery is finished and tear away the stabiliser. Iron out all the wrinkles before stuffing the cushion cover with filling.

18

STAFFORDSHIRE BULL TERRIER

Staffies are some of the most affectionate dogs you will meet,
to the point of blind optimism.

Despite their size, staffies are actually quite long livers –
mostly between 12–14 years old.

MATERIALS

Staffie template   (see page 155)

Sweater (an old or well-worn one
    will be fine)

EQUIPMENT

Sewing machine with free-motion/
    darning foot

Size 60/70 needle

Embroidery bobbin thread

Marker pen

Water-soluble stabiliser,
    such as Sticky Fabri-Solvy

Tear-away stabiliser

30.5-cm (12-in) embroidery hoop

Embroidery scissors

EMBROIDERY THREAD

① #1001 white,
    approximately 54 m (59 yards)

② #1086 off white,
    approximately 18 m (19.7 yards)

③ #1212 light grey,
    approximately 6 m (6.6 yards)

④ #1321 pink,
    approximately 27 m (29.5 yards)

⑤ #1053 blush,
    approximately 11 m (12 yards)

⑥ #1241 charcoal,
    approximately 11 m (12 yards)

⑦ #1000 black,
    approximately 9 m (9.8 yards)

STITCH TECHNIQUES

Straight stitch   (see page 33)

1. Trace the template onto the water-soluble stabiliser (see page 26). It is always best to use both stabilisers when embroidering on knitted garments to prevent over-stretch. Sandwich the sweater between both stabilisers and secure in the embroidery hoop.

2. Straight stitch sections marked ① with thread #1001 white, sections marked ② with thread #1086 off white and sections marked ③ with thread #1212 light grey.

3. Stitch the tongue and mouth sections marked ④ with thread #1321 pink and all sections marked ⑤ with thread #1053 blush, using straight stitch.

4. Straight stitch the nose and eye sections marked ⑥ with thread #1241 charcoal, and lastly sections marked ⑦ with thread #1000 black. Go slowly when stitching these small sections and make sure you fill them up. It is always better to go outside of the lines than to leave small gaps.

5. Once the embroidery is completed, rinse and tear off the stabilisers. Make sure you give the sweater a good press when dry.

19

POMERANIAN

Pomeranians, like other dogs of tiny stature, are seemingly
unaware of their size, often barking at every bigger dog that walks by.

Mozart was so smitten by his pet Pom, Pimperl,
that he dedicated an aria to it.

MATERIALS

Pomeranian template (see page 156)

A plain dress in a non-stretch fabric

EQUIPMENT

Sewing machine with free-motion/
    darning foot

Size 70/80 needle

Embroidery bobbin thread

Marker pen

Tear-away stabiliser

30.5-cm (12-in) embroidery hoop

Embroidery scissors

EMBROIDERY THREAD

① #1055 mid gold,
    approximately 46 m (50 yards)

② #1527 light tan,
    approximately 68 m (74 yards)

③ #1126 dark beige,
    approximately 35 m (38 yards)

④ #1057 mid tan,
    approximately 10 m (11 yards)

⑤ #1321 pink,
    approximately 4 m (4.4 yards)

⑥ #1241 charcoal,
    approximately 2.25 m (2.5 yards)

⑦ #1000 black,
    approximately 4 m (4.4 yards)

⑧ #1001 white,
    approximately 1 m (1 yard)

⑨ #1058 hazel brown,
    approximately 1 m (1 yard)

STITCH TECHNIQUES

Straight stitch (see page 33)

Zigzag stitch (see page 33)

1. Trace the template onto the part of the dress you would like to embroider on (see page 26). Make sure this area is flat and does not have any bulky seams. Add a layer of tear-away stabiliser and secure centrally in the embroidery hoop.

2. Stitch all sections marked ① with thread #1055 mid gold, all sections marked ② with thread #1527 light tan and all sections marked ③ with thread #1126 dark beige, all with zigzag stitch to create texture.

3. Stitch all sections marked ④ with thread #1057 mid tan, with straight stitch.

4. Straight stitch the sections marked ⑤ with thread #1321 pink and the nose section marked ⑥ with thread #1241 charcoal.

5. Using thread #1000 black to straight stitch sections ⑦ and finish off with thread #1001 white for the small eye sections marked ⑧, and finish with #1058 hazel brown for the eyes, marked ⑨.

6. Be very gentle when removing the tear-away stabiliser so it does not damage the dress. Iron the dress with a steam iron.

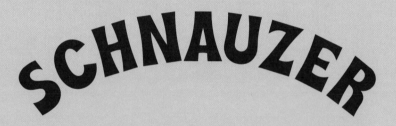

Schnauzers acted as working dogs in World War I;
the German army enlisted them as guard dogs,
while the Red Cross used them as dispatch carriers.

Schnauzers are an incredibly brave and loyal breed.

MATERIALS

Schnauzer template   (see page 157)

Add-on embroideries   (see page 134)

Backpack, approximately 50 x 28 cm
   (20 x 11 in)

EQUIPMENT

Sewing machine with free-motion/
   darning foot

Size 80/90 needle

Embroidery bobbin thread

Marker pen

Water-soluble stabiliser,
   such as Sticky Fabri-Solvy

30.5-cm (12-in) embroidery hoop

Embroidery scissors

EMBROIDERY THREAD

① #1001 white,
   approximately 100 m (109 yards)

② #1118 light blue,
   approximately 50 m (55 yards)

③ #1361 dark grey,
   approximately 30 m (33 yards)

④ #1321 pink,
   approximately 17 m (18.5 yards)

⑤ #1241 charcoal,
   approximately 8 m (8.7 yards)

⑥ #1058 hazel brown,
   approximately 3 m (3.3 yards)

⑦ #1000 black,
   approximately 9 m (9.8 yards)

STITCH TECHNIQUES

Straight stitch   (see page 33)

1. Transfer the template on to the water-soluble stabiliser (see page 26) and attach to front of the backpack with the embroidery hoop.

2. Stitch all sections marked ① with thread #1001 white and all sections marked ② with thread #1118 light blue, using straight stitch. I find it is easier to start with the largest areas first.

3. Straight stitch all sections marked ③ with thread #1361 dark grey.

4. Straight stitch the tongue section marked ④ with thread #1321 pink, the nose section marked ⑤ with thread #1241 charcoal and the eye sections marked ⑥ with thread #1058 hazel brown.

5. Straight stitch all sections marked ⑦ with thread #1000 black.

6. To make this embroidery even more fun, I have added a few embroidered bones around the schnauzer. Please see add-on embroideries (page 134) for template and thread colours.

7. Once you have completed the embroidery, rinse off the stabiliser with lukewarm water and let the bag dry naturally.

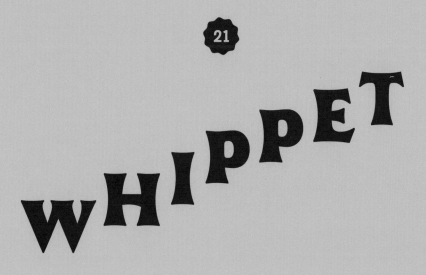

Whippets were traditionally hunting dogs, able to swiftly chase rabbits and game birds.

Despite this, whippets are often regarded as good city dogs, being happy with short bursts of exercise and long naps on the sofa.

MATERIALS

Whippet template   (see page 158)

Navy T-shirt (wash and iron
   before embroidering, in case
   of shrinkage)

EQUIPMENT

Sewing machine with free-motion/
   darning foot

Size 60/70 needle

Embroidery bobbin thread

Water-soluble stabiliser,
   such as Sticky Fabri-Solvy

Tear-away stabiliser

30.5-cm (12-in) embroidery hoop

Embroidery scissors

EMBROIDERY THREAD

① #1212 light grey,
   approximately 43 m (47 yards)

② #1288 mid grey,
   approximately 35 m (38 yards)

③ #1361 dark grey,
   approximately 22 m (24 yards)

④ #1241 charcoal,
   approximately 5 m (5.5 yards)

⑤ #1173 golden amber,
   approximately 1.6 m (1.7 yards)

⑥ #1000 black,
   approximately 2.5 m (2.7 yards)

⑦ #1001 white,
   approximately 1 m (1 yard)

STITCH TECHNIQUES

Straight stitch   (see page 33)

1. Trace the template on to the water-soluble stabiliser (see page 26). It is always best to use both stabilisers when embroidering on a T-shirt as the fabric is very fine and can rip easily. Sandwich the T-shirt between both stabilisers and secure in the embroidery hoop. Make sure the T-shirt is flat but not over-stretched.

2. Straight stitch all sections marked ① with thread #1212 light grey, all sections marked ② with thread #1288 mid grey and all sections marked ③ with thread #1361 dark grey.

3. Stitch the nose section marked ④ with thread #1241 charcoal and eye sections marked ⑤ with thread #1173 golden amber, using straight stitch.

4. Use thread #1000 black to straight stitch sections marked ⑥ and thread #1001 white to straight stitch sections marked ⑦.

5. Once the embroidery is completed, rinse and tear off the stabilisers. Make sure you give the T-shirt a good press when dry.

22

POODLE

Unsurprisingly, there is a reason behind a poodle's often
highly groomed appearance – their fur grows fast, constantly,
and needs regular trims to manage it.

Elvis was a big fan of poodles;
his most well known was called Champagne.

MATERIALS

Poodle template   (see page 159)

T-shirt (wash and iron before
   embroidering, to avoid shrinkage)

EQUIPMENT

Sewing machine with free-motion/
   darning foot

Size 60/70 ballpoint needle

Embroidery bobbin thread

Marker pen

Water-soluble stabiliser,
   such as Sticky Fabri-Solvy

Tear-away stabiliser

30.5-cm (12-in) embroidery hoop

Embroidery scissors

EMBROIDERY THREAD

① #1151 sky grey,
   approximately 89 m (97 yards)

② #1212 light grey,
   approximately 55 m (60 yards)

③ #1118 light blue,
   approximately 18 m (19.7 yards)

④ #1241 charcoal,
   approximately 9 m (9.8 yards)

⑤ #1001 white,
   approximately 24 m (26 yards)

⑥ #1000 black,
   approximately 4.5 m (4.9 yards)

STITCH TECHNIQUES

Straight stitch   (see page 33)

Zigzag stitch   (see page 33)

1. T-shirt fabric is thin and stretchy so both stabilisers should be used. Trace the template on to the water-soluble stabiliser (see page 26) and stick on outer side of T-shirt. Place the tear-away stabiliser on the inside of T-shirt and secure all three layers centrally in the embroidery hoop.

2. Stitch all sections marked ① with thread #1151 sky grey, and all sections marked ② with thread #1212 light grey, both using zigzag stitch.

3. Next, stitch all sections marked ③ with thread #1118 light blue, and sections ④ with thread #1241 charcoal, both using straight stitch.

4. Use thread #1001 white to stitch all sections marked ⑤, using straight stitch.

5. Complete all sections marked ⑥ with thread #1000 black, using straight stitch.

6. When the embroidery is complete, tear off the tear-away stabiliser and rinse off the water-soluble stabilizer with lukewarm water. Dry naturally and press with a steam iron.

COCKER

23

SPANIEL

An American cocker spaniel was the star of the show
in the animated film, *Lady and the Tramp*.

A cocker spaniel isn't the best choice of guard dog, often rolling
on the floor in search of cuddles, such is their affectionate nature.

MATERIALS

Cocker spaniel template (see page 160)

Orange T-shirt

EQUIPMENT

Sewing machine with free-motion/
   darning foot

Size 70/80 ballpoint needle

Embroidery bobbin thread

Marker pen

Water-soluble stabiliser,
   such as Sticky Fabri-Solvy

Tear-away stabiliser

30.5-cm (12-in) embroidery hoop

Embroidery scissors

EMBROIDERY THREAD

① #1361 dark grey,
   approximately 36 m (39 yards)

② #1241 charcoal,
   approximately 45 m (49 yards)

③ #1000 black,
   approximately 36 m (39 yards)

④ #1001 white,
   approximately 11 m (12 yards)

⑤ #1173 golden amber,
   approximately 1.6 m (1.7 yards)

STITCH TECHNIQUES

Straight stitch   (see page 33)

1. Use both water-soluble and tear-away stabiliser when embroidering on to fine, stretchy T-shirt fabric. Trace the template either straight onto the T-shirt or on to the water-soluble stabiliser (see page 26), then secure all layers together in the embroidery hoop.

2. Straight stitch all sections marked ① with thread #1361 dark grey, all sections marked ② with thread #1241 charcoal and all sections marked ③ with thread #1000 black.

3. Use thread #1001 white to straight stitch all sections marked ④ and #1173 golden amber to straight stitch those amazing eyes in sections marked ⑤.

4. Finally, rinse and tear off the stabilisers. Once the T-shirt has dried naturally, press the T-shirt with an iron.

CRICKET THE RESCUE DOG

As a Cypriot rescue dog, Cricket enjoys
nothing more than lying in the sunshine.

Despite being very timid at the beginning,
her inner diva self is now definitely shining through.

MATERIALS

Cricket template   (see page 161)

Black T-shirt (wash and iron before
    embroidering, in case of shrinkage)

EQUIPMENT

Sewing machine with free-motion/
    darning foot

Size 60/70 ballpoint needle

Embroidery bobbin thread

Marker pen

Water-soluble stabilizer,
    such as Sticky Fabri-Solvy

Tear-away stabiliser

30.5-cm (12-in) embroidery hoop

Embroidery scissors

EMBROIDERY THREAD

① #1001 white,
    approximately 45 m (49 yards)

② #1086 off white,
    approximately 21 m (23 yards)

③ #1053 blush,
    approximately 8 m (8.7 yards)

④ #1241 charcoal,
    approximately 23 m (25 yards)

⑤ #1000 black,
    approximately 27 m (29.5 yards)

STITCH TECHNIQUES

Straight stitch   (see page 33)

1. Transfer the template on to water-soluble stabiliser with the marker pen (see page 26). Place on top of the T-shirt with the tear-away stabiliser underneath (I decided to have my embroidery at the back of the T-shirt). Secure centrally in the embroidery hoop.

2. Straight stitch all sections marked ① with thread #1001 white, then all sections marked ② with thread #1086 off white.

3. Cricket has little pink areas around her nose and eyes, so straight stitch these sections marked ③ with thread #1053 blush.

4. Use thread #1241 charcoal to straight stitch sections marked ④ and thread #1000 black to straight stitch sections marked ⑤.

5. Tear or rinse off the stabilisers and let the T-shirt dry. The T-shirt will have creases so give it a good press with a steam iron before wearing.

Add-on Embroideries

Make any of the projects in this book even more special and personal to you by including these add-on embroideries. These are very simple and quick to stitch, so be creative and go wild. You can also resize any of the templates by using a photocopier.

RED LOVE HEART

Embroidery thread

section ①	#1481 Red

Straight stitch

DOUBLE HEART

Embroidery thread

sections ①	#1321 pink
sections ②	#1481 red
sections ③	#1000 black

Straight stitch

BONE

Embroidery thread

sections ①	#1001 white
sections ②	#1000 black

Straight stitch

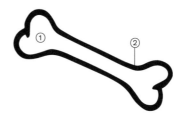

The Templates

BEAGLE

(See page 38)

BOXER

(See page 42)

139

BOSTON TERRIER

(See page 46)

BORDER COLLIE

(See page 50)

GOLDEN RETRIEVER

(See page 54)

BULL TERRIER

(See page 58)

143

CAVALIER
KING
CHARLES

(See page 62)

CHIHUAHUA

(See page 66)

CHOW CHOW

(See page 70)

DACHSHUND

(See page 74)

DALMATIAN

(See page 78)

FRENCH BULLDOG

(See page 82)

PUG

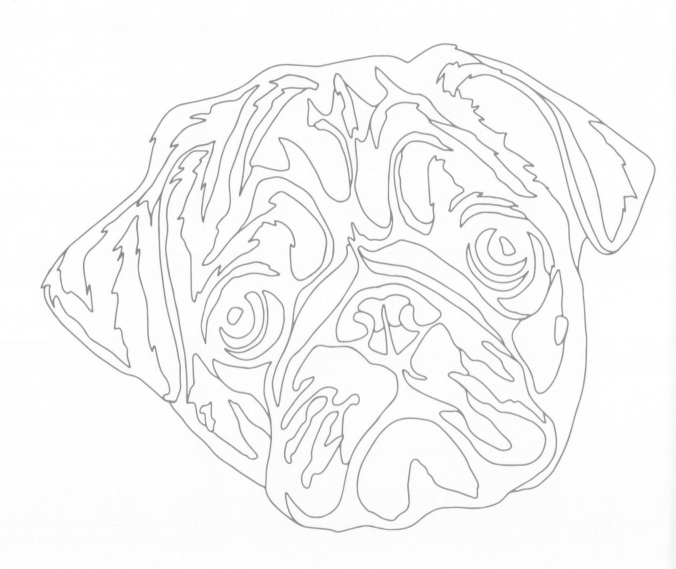

(See page 86)

HUSKY

(See page 90)

ENGLISH BULLDOG

(See page 94)

LABRADOR

(See page 98)

JACK
RUSSELL

(See page 102)

STAFFORDSHIRE BULL TERRIER

(See page 106)

POMERANIAN

(See page 110)

SCHNAUZER

(See page 114)

WHIPPET

(See page 118)

POODLE

(See page 122)

COCKER SPANIEL

(See page 126)

CRICKET
THE
RESCUE
DOG

(See page 130)

About the Author

After completing a fashion design degree in Manchester and spending time living in Glasgow, Carol Tai moved to London to study fabrics and garment-making, and became a creative pattern cutter. Looking for a way to bring her own love of animals and embroidery into her work, she began Hoop n Loop in 2017, to create embroidered pet portraits – inspired by her own dog, Koko.

She recently adopted another puppy, Cricket, who is featured in one of the projects. See what they get up to on Instagram @cricket_tai or check out Carol's pet embroidery work @hoopnloop.

I hope you have enjoyed this book as much as I have enjoyed creating it.

As a huge thank you, I would love to offer you a 20% discount for your very own bespoke dog embroidery.

Check out my website www.hoopnloop.co.uk and use discount code: README20 to redeem your discount.

Carol Tai

Acknowledgements

A massive thank you to everyone who helped behind the scenes and supported me while creating this book. I had so much fun and connected with so many lovely people.

To all the gorgeous dog models, and their beautiful owners who attended the photoshoot. I am so thankful for your patience and willingness to try out almost anything to create the perfect shot – you guys made the extensive four-day photoshoot seemed effortless. Words do not even express my gratitude to you all.

To Eve at Hardie Grant, you reached out to me unexpectedly and inspired me to produce this book. I am thankful for your enthusiasm for Hoop n Loop and glad we shared the same creative vision for the project, making the journey so enjoyable. To Jacqui, who is not a dog photographer, but yet managed to breeze through the shoots to create such beautiful photographs. To the design geniuses, Evi. O and Susan Le, for creating the colourful page layouts.

To my friends, Sara and Eileen, for helping and being there the entire time throughout the photoshoot despite the very early starts and late nights travelling from one side of London to another. I am forever grateful you both gave up your time to help me.

A special thanks to my mum, Joyce, for always being there in my life. For being so understanding and supportive in every decision I make. To the rest of my family for all the joy, laughter and some disagreements throughout the years. To my partner, Paul, who always pushes me to achieve and thrive for more. You have your own special way to cheer me on and always make me laugh through the difficult times with your weird ways.

To my beloved dog, Koko, who has been in our lives for over 10 years and has managed to charm everyone she has ever met. And now to the new member of the family, our rescue dog Cricket. We look forward to living and experiencing new adventures with this special pup.

Finally, to all my friends who have shaped my life in some way or another. I feel very special you are all in my life.

Suppliers

We would like to thank both
of these amazing pet brands
for kindly lending us their
gorgeous dog accessories
for the photoshoot.

A Big
Thank You

HIRO + WOLF

Vibrant British-made pet
accessories

hiro-and-wolf.com

KINTAILS

London-bred dog lifestyle brand,
for designs that are stylish,
functional and expertly fitted

kintails.com

MADEIRA

Embroidery threads

madeira.co.uk

COLORFUL STANDARD

Organic sweaters and T-shirts;
all garments made from 100%
cotton, sustainable, colourful
and uncomplicated

colorfulstandard.co.uk

Index

E

F

G

H

J

Publishing Director: Kate Pollard
Senior Editor: Eve Marleau
Design: Evi. O Studio | Susan Le
Photographer: Jacqui Melville
Prop Stylist: Alexander Breeze
Editor: Gillian Haslam
Proofreader: Sarah Herman
Indexer: Vanessa Bird

Colour reproduction by p2d
Printed and bound in China
by Leo Paper Products Ltd.

Published in 2020 by Hardie Grant Books,
an imprint of Hardie Grant Publishing

Hardie Grant Books (London)
5th & 6th Floors
52-54 Southwark Street
London SE1 1UN

Hardie Grant Books (Melbourne)
Building 1, 658 Church Street
Richmond, Victoria 3121

hardiegrantbooks.com

British Library Cataloguing-in-Publication
Data. A catalogue record for this book
is available from the British Library.

Hoop n Loop by Carol Tai
ISBN: 978-1-78488-372-0

10 9 8 7 6 5 4 3 2 1

JIMINY

JUNO

KEVIN

LLOYD

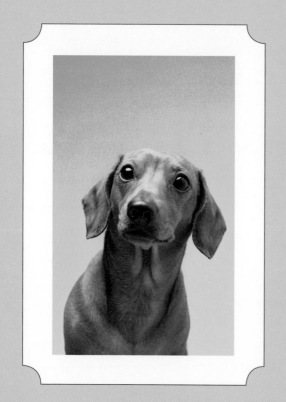

MASH

PEPPA

LELA

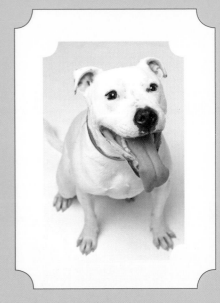

WILBUR

KOKO

WILBUR

BELLA